Fannie Williams McLean, Albert Stanburrough Cook

John Wilson's Prose Style

An undergraduate Thesis

Fannie Williams McLean, Albert Stanburrough Cook

John Wilson's Prose Style
An undergraduate Thesis

ISBN/EAN: 9783337076542

Printed in Europe, USA, Canada, Australia, Japan

Cover: Foto ©ninafisch / pixelio.de

More available books at **www.hansebooks.com**

JOHN WILSON'S

PROSE STYLE

An Undergraduate Thesis

BY

FANNIE W. McLEAN

WITH AN INTRODUCTION

BY

ALBERT S. COOK

Professor of the English Language and Literature in the
University of California

———⁕⁕⁕———

BOSTON

JOHN WILSON'S

PROSE STYLE

An Undergraduate Thesis

BY

FANNIE W. McLEAN

WITH AN INTRODUCTION

BY

ALBERT S. COOK

PROFESSOR OF THE ENGLISH LANGUAGE AND LITERATURE IN THE
UNIVERSITY OF CALIFORNIA

BOSTON
PRINTED BY J. S. CUSHING & CO.
1886

INTRODUCTION.

THE wisdom of printing an undergraduate essay upon the prose of an intellectual giant like Christopher North may not unnaturally be called in question by literary adepts, and the only defence that can be pleaded must either be drawn from custom or sanctioned by a reasonable hope; in other words, must appeal to the past or point confidently to the future. If the theatre of observation be confined to America, it must be admitted that the past is not eloquent in favor of such a proceeding. Here, therefore, it will be necessary to attach credit to those unmistakable signs which herald innovation, and to contemporary events like the issue of the " Johns Hopkins Studies in Historical and Political Science."

In Germany it has long been the rule that dissertations shall be published, and these dissertations are essentially theses for graduation. It would be easy to show that they are the product of the seminaries which are connected with the various departments of the German universities, and that these seminaries, conversely, are the nurseries of original investigation. The relation of the two may best be gathered from an admirable address delivered before the National Educational Association in 1882, by Professor Wright of Dartmouth, and entitled "The Place of Original Research in College Education."

Seminaries akin to those of the German universities have already been instituted in America, and it will be sufficient to refer to a few of the leading ones, such as the linguistic seminaries of Professors March at Lafayette, Allen at Harvard, and Gildersleeve and Warren at Johns Hopkins, or to the historical seminary of Professor C. K. Adams at Michigan, a prototype of the one under Professor H. B. Adams' leadership at Baltimore. But why, it may be asked, should there be seminaries of linguistics and history, and none of literature? Professor Wright justly contends that original research should have the same scope in this subject as in any other. He says:—

"In literature, both ancient and modern, it will rest upon and be conditioned by broad, comprehensive, and accurate reading of original documents, and will consist in analysis, inference, combination of conclusions, independently performed and recorded in carefully written theses, commentaries, or monographs."

The present essay is an attempt to realize this doctrine of original research in its application to literature. The instruction and discipline in English studies received by the writer was shared by her with the members of a class; and she may therefore be considered as a typical senior student of English in the institution of which she was a member. In one sense, it is true, her essay is colored by personal idiosyncrasies, and it would be utterly valueless if it were not. In another, it is devoid of originality, inasmuch as the general mode of treatment and order of topics is that recommended by the example of Minto in his "Manual of English Prose Literature." The only originality to which it pretends is that of due conformity to a method already devised, and of an essential justness, if not profundity of view. That it should lack the robustness, allusiveness, and broad, free handling of its prototype will not be an occasion of wonderment to the initiated, who are aware that these qualities are partly personal, and partly the fruit of wide reading, long experience, and perfect command of literary *technique*. A few verbal errors have been corrected, but I can affirm that in no single instance has the statement of an opinion been modified, or its form materially altered, by my own or any other hand. That the paper has its imperfections and crudities, the writer herself would be the first to avow; but whatever its faults, or whatever its merits, they are to be ascribed solely to herself.

While justification for the hardihood here displayed has been sought in German precedents, that is, in an appeal to the past, may not grounds of extenuation be discovered in a forecast of the future? Should not the production of dissertations and monographs by undergraduate as well as post-graduate students be encouraged? If possessed of sufficient merit, should they not be printed for the instruction, or perhaps warning of others?

For my own part, I see no reason why there might not be a direct friendly interchange of such monographs among the kindred departments of various colleges, or better still, why they should not be distributed by a National Intercollegiate Exchange, established in connection with the Smithsonian Institution, or as an independent agency with officers of its own. There can be little doubt that at present all our colleges are too much isolated, and even their best students too ignorant, in general, of what is occurring at other institutions. But learning, to be truly regenerative, should be cosmopolitan in its entire nature; and to be most amply humanizing and vivific, should be free from the taint of sectionalism and clannishness; it can never fulfil its highest ends, unless it is

> "Whole as the marble, founded as the rock,
> As broad and general as the casing air."

The Germans make university education national, if not cosmopolitan, by encouraging an interchange of intellectual products, producers, and recipients; that is, of learned works, professors, and students. They invoke the aid of a generous rivalry to promote this interchange, thereby stimulating each individual to his greatest intellectual fecundity, and every institution to its highest efficiency. The resulting advantage accrues not only to scholarship, but to the State and the principle of national unity. In one sense the universities have liberated and consolidated Germany, and they certainly tend to perfect that liberation — *Veritas liberabit vos* — and to increase as well the consciousness as the fact of solidarity.

Do our colleges constitute a similar bond, resolving all differences into the harmony of reason, and uniting all educated citizens in the pursuit and realization of a common good? To some extent, it must be conceded, this want is supplied by various societies. We have an Archæological Institute of America, an American Philological Association, one for Social Science, another for Physical Science, and still another for Modern Languages. All of these depend, professedly or indirectly, upon the colleges. But why should there not be even the semblance of unity among the colleges as such? And, supposing such unity desirable, would not one step towards it be taken by the increase of original investigation in all departments, the publication of its results, though confessedly crude, and a freer circulation of the monographs among the sister colleges of the land?

Nor would the reflex gain to the individual college be insignificant. The honor of being selected for the noble task of augmenting human knowledge would be eagerly sought for by the most highly gifted, energetic, and unselfish students, and the more ordinary incentives of prizes, scholarships, and Commencement honors might be withdrawn, so completely would they be outshone by the more brilliant reward of application, the permission to serve one's *Alma Mater*, one's country, and one's race, the privilege of communicating to a sympathetic audience what had been achieved by severe toil, yet with the buoyancy begotten of magnanimous resolve and a yet undaunted hope.

That these imaginings are not altogether baseless I would fain believe, and am indeed partly convinced; and it is because of my conviction that this little essay is sent forth upon the world.

ALBERT S. COOK.

BERKELEY, CALIFORNIA,
February 22, 1886.

JOHN WILSON.

1785–1854.

LIFE.

JOHN WILSON, more familiarly known in literature as Christopher North, was born in Paisley, a manufacturing town of Scotland, on the 18th of May, 1785, and died on the 2d of April, 1854. The most reliable and interesting account of his life is given in the work entitled *A Memoir of John Wilson*, compiled from family papers and other sources by his daughter, Mrs. Gordon.

His life, for the most part, was uninterrupted in its smooth and even course. There are but few occurrences which seem to have any special prominence. Its history, as bearing on his literary work, may be divided into three periods. The first is the period of poetry, when his youthful genius, spurred on by the consciousness of intellectual power, and excited by the passion of love, expressed itself in smooth and tender lines. The second period originates with the birth of *Blackwood's Magazine*, where, for the first time, Christopher North found a fitting arena for his literary feats. The third period dates from the death of his wife, which occurrence so deeply affected his nature, as to cast its shadow on all his future writings.

(1) The father of John Wilson was a well-to-do gauze manufacturer; his mother, a lady of high birth, who gave to her son a goodly heritage of wit, humor, and wisdom, combined with physical beauty and grace. The loveliness of the natural scenery around his early home is described by him in *Fytte First of Christopher in his Sporting Jacket*. When a child he was a miniature Professor Wilson and Christopher North in one; for we find him in his seventh year preaching sermons, witty and pathetic, to his brothers and sisters, and, when even younger, amusing himself by fishing.

Some happy school-days, apostrophized by him in his *Soliloquy on the Seasons*, were passed in the parish of Mearns. Here he took the lead in school-work, as well as in out-door sports. From the year 1797 to 1803 he attended Glasgow College, where his time was equally and successfully divided between work and pleasure. During these days he kept a unique diary, called a common-place book, which he continued for many years; and evinced other traits of regularity and punctuality afterwards erased from the character of Christopher North. At the age of seventeen he was distinguished as being the best-read fellow in college. Among his early friends were Alexander Blair, Robert Findlay, William Dunlop, and Archibald Hamilton.

In 1804 Wilson entered Oxford as a gentleman-commoner of Magdalen College. The results of his systematic and enthusiastic study were displayed in the honorable examinations he passed, and later, in his keen and accurate writings. At this time his common-place book contains essays, critical and imaginative, which display many characteristics embryonic of the future

Christopher North. Aside from his scholarly attainments while at college, his talent for brilliant conversation and forcible debate, and his skill in all athletic sports, made him the centre of a host of admiring friends. His first illustrious success as a scholar was made in the brilliant examination he passed in 1807 for the Bachelor degree. This ended his university life.

In 1807 he settled in Elleray, a beautiful cottage on Lake Windermere, in that country which was the retreat of so many celebrated authors, — De Quincey, Coleridge, Wordsworth, and Southey. Here his life was one of poetic meditation, of sociability, and of out-door recreation. In 1807 his common-place book contains the poems, *The Isle of Palms* and *The Angler's Tent*. In 1811 John Wilson was married to Jane Penny, a beautiful and accomplished lady, with whom he passed twenty-eight years of wedded happiness. His first volume of poems, containing the *Isle of Palms*, was published in 1812, and was received with but little enthusiasm. Poetry was evidently not the mode in which Wilson's thoughts could best be presented to the world. His second volume, *The City After the Plague, and Other Poems*, was published in 1816.

The loss of his fortune compelled him, in 1815, to leave his home in Elleray, and to move with his family to Edinburgh. He was now admitted to the Bar, but as a lawyer gained little success. The vacations of his profession he spent in climbing and in fishing among the Highlands of Scotland, and meanwhile gathered together the materials for his *Recreations*.

(2) Christopher North was first introduced to the world in the pages of *Blackwood's Magazine* in 1817.

North was an imaginative character, under whose cloak and behind whose crutch Wilson disguised himself from the public. Periodical literature was better adapted than poetry to the versatility of his powers and to his peculiar temperament. The years 1810–32 were the scene of a bitter political controversy in Scotland. The *Edinburgh Review* was the organ of the Whig party, and *Blackwood's* the organ of the Tory party. Until 1817 the *Edinburgh Review* had been the only periodical of any importance, and had consequently held undisputed sway. But now a formidable rival arose in this new magazine. In its pages Christopher North poured forth a rich stream of ideas on politics, poetry, philosophy, religion, art, books, men, and nature. His first articles, written in the flush of political excitement, show a violence of language, and a mercilessness in satire, which were afterwards abandoned by him without any loss of strength or pungency, and with a great gain in accuracy.

In 1820 John Wilson offered himself as a candidate for the chair of Moral Philosophy made vacant by the death of Dr. Thomas Brown. His opponents were Sir William Hamilton, James Mackintosh, and Mr. Malthus. Wilson was finally appointed professor, and continued in the chair until his resignation a few years previous to his death. His lectures on philosophy, described by his students as masterpieces of brilliant rhetoric, sound logic, and deep argument, have never been printed. He received the admiration and profound love of these students. "To them he was Der Einzige. They *felt* philosophy. The mental faculties were no mere names; the passions, affections, and dread mysteries of conscience ceased to be abstract matters of speculation, and were exhibited before them as living and solemn realities mirrored in their own kindling hearts."

The duties of Wilson the professor did not check the flow of North's contributions to *Blackwood's*. Many times nearly the whole magazine was of his composition. In 1822 *The Lights and Shadows of Scottish Life* was published. These tales are designated as poems in prose, and Mr. Field asserts that they are "the most perfect example of their kind of story in our language." From this time until 1837 his life was one of intense and persevering labor, of strict devotion to literary and philosophical work and study. During the year 1826 his contributions to *Blackwood's* were no less than twenty-seven articles, among which were *Cottages, Streams, Meg Dods* and *Gymnastics*. In 1828 his most important essays were *Christopher in his Sporting Jacket, Old North and Young North, Christmas Dreams, Health and Longevity, Salmonia* and *Sacred Poetry*.

To the year 1831 belongs his essay on *Homer and his Translators*, which scholars say "contains the most vivid and genial criticisms in our own or any other language." The same year saw his criticism on Tennyson, who was then but a young poet of uncertain fame.

1833 and 1834 were years of political excitement in Edinburgh, so Christopher North, who was always interested in current affairs, appeared in many political essays. The summer of 1834 Wilson spent with his family in the Ettrick Forest. His wife, his children, and his pets form the oft-recurring themes of the beautiful imaginative essays written at that time. In September of this year Blackwood died. Wilson was obliged to perform a prodigious amount of writing in order to bring out the next number of the magazine. Of its one hundred and forty-two pages, fifty-six were from his pen. These included *A Glance at the Noctes of Athenaeus* and a *Review of Coleridge's Poetical Works*.

(3) The death of his wife in 1837 not only made a deep impression on his sensitive nature, but also gave a grave, more subdued cast, to all his writings, which were so truly the mirror of his feelings. At this period of his life we find a moderation in his political views.

After his wife's death, Wilson's writings were less numerous. His only article for *Blackwood* in 1840 was a *Review of a Legend of Florence by Leigh Hunt*. In this same year, after communication with different acquaintances of Burns, and an examination of his history from all possible testimonies, Christopher North wrote a just and delicate account of that poet's life. This was published by Messrs. Blackie of Glasgow in *The Land of Burns*. Four years later he took a prominent part in the Burns Festival.

In 1845 he wrote a *Criticism of Macaulay's Lays of Ancient Rome*, the first article since 1840. After this there was another period of silence, until, in 1848, he criticized, in the magazine, *Byron's Address to the Ocean*. In 1847 he was elected first president of the Philosophical Institute in Edinburgh, and was re-elected every year until his death.

In 1849 the first of a series of ten papers, entitled *Dies Boreales*, were seen in the pages of *Blackwood*. They were early recognized to be the work of the same hand that penned the *Noctes*, but consisted of more mature and more connected discussions on great moral questions, and criticisms of some of the masterpieces of literature.

In the winter of 1850 Wilson's strong physical constitution first began to show the marks of old age in a paralytic stroke. In the summer of the following year he took a trip through the Highlands, but there was no improvement in his health. On his return he tendered his resignation of the chair of Philosophy, and thus passed from active service. As a proof of the great esteem in which he was held, the queen granted him a pension of three hundred pounds a year. The last production of his pen were numbers nine and ten of *Dies Boreales* for *Blackwood*. The remaining years of his life present a gratifying picture of a peaceful and happy old age. As an example of his independence in political views, and of his magnanimity of spirit, we note this little incident. In 1852 he arose from his sick-bed in order to cast his vote for Macaulay, his old Whig antagonist, as a representative to Parliament. The gradual weakening of his wonderful mental and physical powers culminated in 1854, when this noble man and distinguished scholar died.

CHARACTER.

Personal Appearance. — The fine physical appearance of John Wilson has formed the subject of many a beautiful engraving and of many a fine word-picture. Lockhart, his co-conspirator of *Blackwood's*, describes him thus: "His hair is of the true Sicambrian yellow; his eyes are of the brightest, and at the same time of the clearest blue; and the blood glows in his cheek with as firm a fervor as it did, according to the description of Jornandes, in those of the *Bello-gaudentes, praelio-videntes Teutones* of Attila." Samuel Warren, in his *Personal Recollections of North*, gives this account of his impressions on first seeing Wilson. His excited exclamations remind us of Wilson himself. "When he came near enough for his face to be seen with distinctness, I forgot everything else about him: and I shall never forget the impression it produced. What a magnificent head! How firmly chiselled his features! What a compression of the thin, but beautifully formed lips! What a bright-blue flashing 'Eye, like Mars, to threaten or command,' flowing auburn hair, and the erect, commanding set of his head upon his shoulders; and surely, no Grecian sculptor could have desired anything beyond it." His voice, too, was an index to his character. It is described as deep and sad, with a nervous tremor. In Faed's beautiful engraving of Sir Walter Scott and his Friends, the magnificent form of Professor Wilson is leaning over the chair of the great novelist.

The strength, beauty, and vigor of his physical body was transmitted to his literary offspring. In respect to both he was a Hercules-Apollo. This splendid animalism clung to him almost to the very end of life, and he never lost the peculiar commanding bearing of his noble figure.

Activity. — Wilson was a man, who, physically and mentally, was ever on the alert. There are many curious stories told of his wonderful walking feats, his pugilistic encounters, his athletic sports and fishing excursions. He interested himself in all the domestic concerns of his own home, and in the affairs of his friends. His recreations were always of an active nature. His travelling was confined almost entirely to the country, and it is somewhat surprising that a man of the world, such as he, cared so little for city life. Very few were his visits to London. He dashed off these lines to describe his feelings on first beholding that great city: "Now were we in the eddies,—the vortices,—the whirlpools of the great roaring sea of life! and away we were carried, not afraid, yet somewhat trembling in the awe of our new delight, into the heart of the habitations of all the world's most imperial, most servile, most tyrannous, and most slavish passions! All that was most elevating and most degrading, most startling and most subduing too; most trying by temptation of pleasure, and by repulsion of pain; into the heart of all joy and all grief; all calm and all storm; all dangerous trouble and more dangerous rest; all rapture and all agony — crime, guilt, misery, madness, despair."

The mind of this author rivalled his body in the constant activity of its powers. Every subject of the day was quickly revolved in his mind, and room made for the next. Little time was spent in day-dreaming. Even his reminiscences are not simple recollections of the past, but are interwoven with many new thoughts and fancies.

In the history of his life we have noted the almost inconceivable amount of literary work performed by him for *Blackwood*. Eight thousand two hundred and thirty-four pages of that magazine were contributed by his pen. These articles were written from enthusiastic love of composition, for the pecuniary reward was slight. He said that he did more work for "Maga" with less pay than any other contributor. Added to this literary labor were the arduous duties of his professorship. Wilson indeed proved that to live earnestly is to live well.

Sensuous Nature.—The sensuous framework of Wilson's being was most delicately fashioned. In the presence of nature he was always filled with silent awe. It was not until this first feeling had passed away that he gave utterance to his beautiful apostrophes to nature, in which he "animates the insensate earth, till she speaks, smiles, laughs, weeps, sighs, groans, goes mad and dies." The poet soul of Wilson delighted in midnight wanderings, when in the silence all around him he drank into his very being the mystery and beauty of nature. Not only was his eye sensitive to all beauty, but, like De Quincey, he possessed a peculiarly sensitive ear, alive to every sound of music. We find *Christopher in the Aviary* describing with delicate appreciation the songs of various birds. Nor did Wilson deem it degrading to pamper that other sense,—the taste. From his essay, *Christopher at the Lakes*, we quote this luscious description of a meal in a Highland cottage:—"Such bread! baked of finest flour for the nonce in a pan-oven that raises the light brown crust almost into the delicacy of the coating of bride-cake, while close-grained even as that 'mighty magic,' *kythes*, as you break it, the crumbling inconsistency of the fair interior! Graceful from the gridiron that crump circle of oatmeal wafers, broad as the bottom of a bee-hive; and what honeycomb! The scent is as of thyme, and, by some conjuration, preserved has been the cellular framework all winter through, and therein lies the dewy flower-distilment, as clear as when the treasure was taken at harvest-close from the industrious people, who in a moment hushed their hum. That is *our* pot of porridge; and oh! it is exquisite when supped with cream!... Aren't these pretty patterns of suns and sunflowers, stars and roses, impressed on the glistening countenance of that glorious butter? Till now never saw we yellow. Put a spoon into that cream — it stands for a few moments straight — and then slowly declining, leans on the edge of the jug, like a young lady about to go into a swoon."

Characteristics of Writings. — The two most marked characteristics of Wilson's literary work are: (1) The great variety of subjects treated with equal power and facility; and (2) the unparalleled number of his productions.

(1) The variety of subjects is accounted for by the fact that he took a zealous interest in every branch of human life and knowledge; hence the profuse and varied flow of his thoughts. The almost necessary expression in words of this constant overflux of ideas precluded, whether regrettably or otherwise, the writing of any one sustained work. It is doubtful whether the sparkle of his wit, the tenderness of his pathos, the strength of his sublimity, the subtlety of his thought, could all have been crystallized into one great work. Such a production would indeed have been a masterpiece of transcendent literary art; but, rather than lose any of his gracious spontaneity, we might well prefer these exquisite fragments of an ununited whole. In these papers from *Blackwood* he re-animates the stirring political times of the past; he gives us his per-

sonal estimate of his national literature, and sheds the light of his genius upon all things, great and trivial, of his day.

We have already intimated by the title Hercules-Apollo that Wilson possessed both strength and beauty. He was poet, philosopher, and critic in one. When we call him a poet we have reference to the poetry in his prose. In his poems, such as *The Isle of Palms*, the exuberance of his thought seems to be unnaturally checked by the necessity for rhyme and metre. He is, in truth, more poetical when he pours forth his sparkling thoughts unrestrainedly, in words tearful with pathos, laughing with humor, and grand in their earnestness. It has been remarked of his prose "that he approached more nearly than any modern since Burke to that wild prophetic movement of style which the bards of Israel exhibit; nay, more nearly even than Burke, since with Wilson it is a perpetual afflatus." All these beautiful fancies are wrought by a brain, not excited with opium, as with De Quincey, but in its normal, healthy condition.

Wilson was not only a poetical rhapsodist, but also a sound, deep thinker; his mind was powerful to grapple with grave subjects. Side by side with a tender reminiscence of some childhood scene is a thoughtful and logical paper on *Education*, or on *The Punishment of Death*. Moreover, his versatile genius led him to treat of the same theme in different ways,— at one time in a pathetic strain, at another, in a humorous.

(2) The ease and rapidity with which he wrote form an explanation of the great number of his literary works. In a few hours he could write what would have

taken another author as many days. The systematic and carefully prepared work performed during the early part of his career was entirely superseded by his later hurried and careless production, described by him in the *Noctes:* " We love to do our work by fits and starts. We hate to keep fiddling away, an hour or two at a time, at one article for weeks. So off with our coat, and at it like a blacksmith. When we once get the way of it, hand over hip, we laugh at Vulcan and all his Cyclops. From nine of the morning till nine at night, we keep hammering away at the metal, iron or gold, till we produce a most beautiful article. A biscuit and a glass of Madeira, twice or thrice at the most, and then to a well-won dinner. In three days, gentle reader, have we, Christopher North, often produced a whole magazine, — a most splendid number. For the next three weeks we were as idle as a desert, and as vast as an antre; and thus on we go, alternately laboring like an ant, and relaxing in the sunny air like a dragon-fly, enamored of extremes." His youthful, pains-taking labor blossomed in the smooth, even, neatly-laid lines of his poetry, while we find, as the outcome of his later mode of writing, an unequal prose structure, composed of many varieties of material, from the coarsest of clay to the most precious of stones. In these irregularities, his prose may be contrasted with the uniform richness and stately dignity of Macaulay, and with the smooth precision of Addison. Nevertheless, breadth of treatment must not be erroneously confounded with shallowness. On the contrary, Wilson pierces at once down to the very centre of a subject with a true philosophic eye. The truth he finds there beats like a heart, out of sight, underneath a body of delicate, stylistic beauty.

The underlying stratum of all Wilson's qualities was his broad sympathy. His works are said to be *sui generis* and inimitable. They are so from their essential vitality, from the presence of Christopher himself in all he writes. He felt, he saw, he studied everything intensely. His warm sympathies, his heart-wholeness and earnestness, pervade the pages of his essays. He surpasses all writers in his exhaustless store of vivid boyhood reminiscences.

Wilson's loyalty to his own people, and to his own order (he professed to belong to the working order), gave him great popularity and influence. From his boyhood this "gay, girt-hearted fellow," was a favorite among all classes. Although his brilliant conversational powers and fine personal appearance gave him entrance into the highest circles of society, he was more often to be found at his own hearth-stone, in the public inn, or in the dwellings of his humbler friends. He was thoroughly Scotch in nature, as was Walter Scott; but the works of both these great men are read in other countries with the same relish as in their own. The *Noctes* have met with even greater popularity in America than in Scotland.

The alleged vanity of Wilson is purely a fiction, as much a product of his imaginative brain as the crutch of old Christopher in the *Noctes*. In reality, he was humble and unselfish in disposition; simple, eloquent, earnest, and vigorous. His eloquence was no affected brilliancy; it was the steadily-burning flame of the fire within.

A strong magnetism is possessed by his writings,— a power to impassion, to excite a noble rapture. This magnetic influence was felt particularly by the members of his class in philosophy. His most admirable characteristic was his mastery over the hearts of the young. Mr. Field pronounces him a "teacher of youth, who gloried in the God-given power of imparting knowledge to the young and ardent."

OPINIONS.

Political. — Wilson, though thoroughly loyal to Scotland, was imbued with broad English views, on account of his long residence in that country. During the most vigorous years of his life, political warfare was raging in Great Britain. Wilson was a Tory and strongly conservative; he upheld existing institutions, and believed, not in sudden revolutions, but in gradual reformations; he was an opponent of the Reform Bill of 1832, and a staunch supporter of Free Trade. The urgencies of the time made it necessary for a man of his frank and upright nature to express his sentiments boldly on the one side or the other. However, his liberty of thought caused him to differ from the Tories in certain respects. He was a firm advocate of the education of all classes, and has written an argumentative and defensible paper on that subject. The following is his opinion regarding the effects of educating the lower classes: — "Let not men — the men of this great and free country — fear the ultimate effects of knowledge. It is a great power poured in, and will produce some commotion; but will settle and find its way to its proper places. The immediate effects are not the ultimate. At first a degree of emotion is excited, which belongs not to the matter, but to the times — the novelty, the suddenness, the generality, namely, the act of diffusion. But the lasting impressions are those which belong to the matter. Nothing is without risk — nothing great at least. But neither is it without risk to do nothing — to leave everything alone. Certain it is that the Old World has greatly and suddenly changed. One thing is true, that injurious and corrupt abuse will not stand before an enlightened people — nor ought it. The instruction of the people will give a tenfold, but not a turbulent weight to public opinion. The danger is, not from knowledge or reason, but from the concurrence of particular changes of opinion with particular causes of political ferment, which may or may not happen. It has been confessed that Intellect has causes of disturbance, but that they are tempered and subdued by morality. Let there be sufficient causes of the morality of the people, and Intellect will not hurt them; let there not be, and Intellect will not be wanted to make mischief."

Wilson carried the burden of his people's troubles upon his large heart, and considered it his duty to point out to them that their weal was further advanced, and their manhood better honored, by a steady perseverance in their rural duties, than by mingling in the fierce political frays of the time. It was his aim to show to them the beauties of their country life. In writing to De Quincy, he says of the *Lights and Shadows of Scottish Life:* "I have wished to speak of humble life, and the elementary feelings of the human soul in isolation, under the light of a veil of poetry." A division of ranks in society he considered inevitable, but a disparity in their worth and importance impossible.

Critical. — Wilson was the critical autocrat of his generation. Among his critical works are essays on *Homer*, *The Greek Drama*, *Greek Anthology*, *The Hindoo Drama*, six essays on *Spenser*, his *Specimens of the British Critics*, and portions of the *Dies Boreales*. He introduced a peculiar kind of criticism in which there is no attempt at brilliant originality, in which the author does not make himself the central figure, but the author criticized. He produces this result by an entire lack of the flowery adornment and playful egotism characteristic of his other works. The simplicity of his style causes us to forget the interpreter and brings us into immediate contact with the author. We call Wilson an interpreter because his criticism of others consists in interpretations of their thoughts and feelings.

It was Wilson's desire to make the name of Wordsworth loved and renowned, and with this intent he wrote often in praise of his favorite poet. When a boy at college he had read Wordsworth's *Lyrical Ballads*, and so great was his admiration for them that he immediately wrote a letter of thanks to the poet. In this letter there was noticeable in the youthful critic a nice power of discrimination, which detected faults even in the hero he worshipped. He intimates to Wordsworth that there are some subjects so repugnant to our feelings as to be unfit themes for a poet. Of such was the story of the *Idiot Boy*. At this time Wordsworth was but an obscure poet, and Wilson was among the first critics to notice him favorably. In after years his laudations of the Lake poet were many, but never exaggerated. He accuses him of a lack of warm religious sentiments in *The Excursion*, presumably a religious poem.

In a second characteristic Wilson's criticisms differed from many others, in their unswerving aim at truthfulness. No critical remark was made without careful forethought. He directed all the keen arrows of his wit against the many critics who touch with ruthless hands those works which should be to them objects of reverence. We have already spoken of the careful study of Burns' life and works he made in order to set that much abused poet before the world in the light of truth. These are the words of the shepherd in one of the *Noctes:* "I canna conceive a mair sacred, a mair holy task, than that which a man takes upon himsel, when he sits doun to write the life and character of his brither man. Afore he begins to write the capital letter at the beginnin o' the first word, he ocht to hae sat mony a lang hour, a' by himsel, in his study, and to hae walked at eventide mony a lang hour, a' by himsel, alang the flowings of some river (hoo life-like!) — and to hae lain awake during mony a lang hour, a' by himsel, and to hae lain awake during mony a lang hour o' the night-watches, *and especially then a' by himsel* — meditating on the duty he has undertaken to perform, and comparing or contrasting, as it may be, what he *may conjecture* to hae been the character o' his brither, whom God has called to judgment, wi' what he *must ken* to be the character o' his ain sel', whom God next moment may call to his dread account." This desire for truthfulness causes him to be particular rather than general in his criticisms; as, for example, in *A Few Words on Thomson.*

Philosophic. — As to Wilson's scientifically philosophic opinions, unfortunately we can give no accurate account, as none of his lectures on philosophy have been published. We do not know to what particular school he belonged, nor what were his explanations of the leading problems whose solution enters into all philosophy. From the many beautiful and subtle philosophical speculations in his essays we notice a tendency towards Pure Idealism. His words and deeds testify to his belief in the immense responsibility of life, in the immortality of the soul, in God, and in his revealed Word. The question he asked concerning Robert Burns, "Did he read the Bible?" can be answered in the affirmative of Wilson. That Book was to him "even as the sky — with its sun, moon, and stars, its boundless blue with all its cloud-mysteries — its peace deeper than the grave, because of realms beyond the grave, — its tumult louder than that of life, because heard altogether in all the elements." His arguments for the immortality of the soul seem to proceed from the feelings, and to have instinctive convictions for their authority rather than logical reasoning.

Wilson, like Macaulay, was an optimist. There was nothing in his nature akin to the misanthrope who complains of the vanity and coldness of this world, and of its slight appreciation of genius. He believed that all genius receives its reward here, that the world is warm and beautiful if men's hearts are so, that all is good excepting our sin, that there is not even such a thing as bad weather, for " tho' we may na be able to see, we can aye think o' the clear blue lift." In short, his philosophy, summed up in one sentence, is this: — "Do your duty to God and man, and fear not that, when that dust dies, the spirit that breathed by it will live forever."

ELEMENTS OF STYLE.

VOCABULARY.

Copiousness and flexibility of diction are natural antecedents to great variety in literary production. Consequently we find these two qualities noticeably present in Wilson's writings. In the prodigality and splendor of his words he rivals Carlyle, though not in the coining of original words. Like Carlyle, in spite of his wonderful command over a profuse vocabulary, he sometimes delights in the repetition of words which, from their sound or associations, have pleased his fancy. This expression occurs very frequently in his essays, "winnowing the air with their wings." His mercurial disposition, the suddenness with which one feeling followed another in his heart and one picture another in his brain, necessitated the same quick transitions in his diction. Therefore a poetical and musical flow of words is followed by some slang phrase of the day, or by some rare Scottish expression. Thus is displayed to us an endless kaleidoscopic variety.

In general Wilson's vocabulary consists more in words of Anglo-Saxon derivation than in those of Latin. Yet he is not such a purist in this respect as is De Quincey in the use of Latin derivatives. The prevalence of these hardy English words gives to his style strength and homeliness, an effect, however, somewhat counteracted by the picturesque and musical nature of his expressions.

In discussing Wilson's vocabulary we divide it into three classes: (1) *Classical* or *Standard English*, (2) *Scotticisms*, (3) *Outlawed English*.

(1) His classical English is composed of the most expressive and most musical words in our language. He scatters them most lavishly in his descriptions of Highland scenery and in his stories of Highland life. From this fact we discover that he was more intimately acquainted with the objective than with the subjective side of our language, and in this respect differs from De Quincey. Even in speaking of the human feelings, he, by means of figures of speech, still clings to words descriptive of sensible objects. An example of this tendency, and also of the delicate subtlety of his language, is his description of the different ways in which a poet may affect the human heart: —

"You may infuse the sentiment by a single touch — by a ray of light no thicker, nor one thousandth part so thick, as the finest needle ever silk-threaded by lady's finger; or you may dance it in with a flutter of sunbeams; or you may splash it in as with a gorgeous cloud-stain stolen from sunset; or you may bathe it in with a shred of the rainbow. Perhaps the highest power of all possessed by the sons of song is to breathe it in with the breath, to let it slip in with the light of the common day!"

In his word-pictures Wilson uses many felicities of speech characteristic of a poet. He seems to slip naturally into alliteration. On almost every page are examples of this poetical device. Sometimes, even, he adds rhyme to alliteration in the poetical fragments of his prose. Bits of word-coloring are suggestive of the old ballad singers.

To Wilson's creative mind belong many original combinations of words in the form of compound adjectives. He uses these with great effect not only in his imaginative, but also in his critical essays. A whole critical analysis is condensed into these few words: "Common-manners-painting poetry of Crabbe, dark-passion-painting poetry of Byron, high-romance-painting poetry of Scott." There is no trace of a Critical Terminology in these essays. His versatile and original genius needed no such aid. But there is a direct aim at strength and simplicity of language, which resulted oftentimes in such expressive epithets as this, "Scott the great magician."

His inexhaustible wealth of words is also manifest in the frequent artifice of accumulated adjectives. Ten or twelve adjectives, describing the same noun, and each with but a shade's difference in meaning from the preceding, follow each other to a perfect climax. "Is not spring, at times, the gladdest, gayest, gentlest, mildest, meekest, modestest, softest, sweetest, and sunniest of all God's creatures that steal along the face of the earth."

The too capricious use of these accumulated adjectives tends to weaken the force of his thought by diluting rather than concentrating its energies.

(2) Wilson's consummate skill in handling the Scottish language gives to his writings their most exquisite and inimitable charm. It is the language of Burns and of Scott. They have immortalized it in their pages, where it will still exist after it has ceased to be a spoken language. Wilson wields it with still more natural ease, with a richer copiousness and splendor, than did even these two masters of the language. The dialect of the shepherd in the *Noctes* is so thoroughly Scotch, that, if Anglicized, its raciness could not be preserved.

His is not a provincial dialect, but the true burry speech of the old Scot. The same characteristics that belong to Wilson's classical English belong to this Scotch.

(3) We apply the term outlawed English to the slang phrases, coarse expressions, puns, and colloquialisms which mar the beauty and sweetness of Wilson's diction. They can only seem excusable when we appreciate that many of his writings were of the nature of familiar conversations with the readers of *Blackwood*, and that he was of necessity brought into close contact with people of all classes. Such words as the following are not legitimate in any work of art: "slang-whangishness," "pully-hawlying," "plump-down," "sparker," "make themselves scarce." His brilliant genius alone saves his literary productions from irrevocable degradation by his familiarity with common speech.

SENTENCES.

The sentences of Wilson's prose may best be designated as loose in arrangement and irregular in construction. The proof of this statement is obtained by an examination of those works most peculiarly his own, the *Noctes* and the *Recreations*. His strictly critical essays are an exception in this respect, as they were in their vocabulary. They differed from his other compositions in the simplicity of their diction, as they likewise differ in the regularity of their sentence structure, which is built up, for the most part, of sentences either simple, or, if complex, with but few modifying clauses, and these in exact grammatical order. To vary the monotony there is occasionally the interspersion of periodic sentences. Through the medium of such nicely compacted sentences Wilson attained the clearness for which he sought in his formal criticisms.

But for typical examples we must look in the greater bulk of his writings. Here the sentences display a general unconformity to all grammatical and rhetorical rules.

The periodic sentence is uncommon with Wilson. When this form of sentence is used, the suspension is brought about by introducing the sentence with an adjective. "Sweet would be the hush of lake, woods, and skies, were it not so solemn." "Beautiful is it by nature, with its bays, and fields, and woods." Such sentences are constructed not for the sake of holding and heightening the interest, but to emphasize the adjective, which was always an expressive and potent word with Wilson. Of the true periodic sentence there is no instance. Sometimes the climax is found in the middle of the sentence, but it is never pushed forward to the end. The hurrying spontaneity of his thought suggests new ideas which must be crowded into the same sentence, even after a proper close has been reached. In the following sentence, apparently we have grasped the significance of his thought when we arrive at the word "transfigured." However, he adds another succession of clauses after the predicate: —

"Therefore bad as boys too often are — and a disgrace to the mother who bore them — the cradle in which they were rocked — the nurse by whom they were suckled — the school-master by whom they were flogged — and the hangman by whom it was prophesied they were to be executed — wait patiently for a few years, and you will see them all transfigured — one into a preacher of such winning eloquence, that he almost persuades all men to be Christians — another into a parliamentary orator, who commands the applause of listening senates," etc. Enough of the sentence has been quoted to illustrate the point. The periodic style was unnatural to Wilson's play of mind, in which thought was joined to thought by an emotional, and not by a logical link. He trusted to the intrinsic interest of the subject-matter, and to the glowing eloquence of his language, rather than to any formal sentence artifices to attract the attention of his readers. The sentence forms into which he naturally slipped were of a nature foreign to the period.

Wilson's most characteristic sentences are either abruptly short or extremely long. In the latter, one co-ordinate statement is heaped upon another. This same tendency in Carlyle's writings was denominated by Minto "a studied ruggedness and a careless cumulative method." In Wilson, however, it is not studied, but natural. Especially do we note these constructions in his descriptions of natural scenery, where his strong feelings sweep him beyond the pale of rhetorical rules. Many sentences in the *Recreations* are three or four pages in length; he clusters one picture around another as if he knew not when to cease drawing from the crowded art-gallery of his imagination. These lengthy cumulative sentences are not confined solely to his descriptions of nature. He often employs them in argumentative discourses, in narration, in fact whenever his excited feelings have the mastery over his pen. As a fine example of these long sentences we quote from the *Noctes*: —

"Hunt the dew-drops after they have fled from before the sun-rising — the clouds that have gone sailing away over the western horizon, to be in at the sun-setting — the flashing and foaming waves that have left the sea and all her isles in a calm at last — the cushats still murmuring on farther and farther into the far forest, till the sound is now faint as an echo, and then nothing — golden eagles lost in light, and raging in their joy on the very rim of this globe's attraction — during the summer heats, the wild flowers that strew the old woods of Caledon only during the pure snowy breath of the earth-brightening spring — the stars, that at once disappear with all their thousands, at the howl of the midnight storm — the lightnings suddenly intersecting the collied night, and then off and away forever, quicker than forgotten thoughts — the grave-mounds, once so round and green, James, and stepped over so tenderly by footsteps going towards the low door of the little kirk, but all gone now, James, — kirk, kirk-yard, and all, James, — and not a house in all the whole parish that has not been many times over and over again pulled down — altered — rebuilt, till a ghost, could he but loosen himself from the strong till, and raise up his head from among a twenty-acre field of turnips, and potatoes, and pease, would not know his own bonny birth-place, and death-place too, once so fringed and fragrant with brushwood over all its knolls, with whins, and broom, and harebells, and in moist moorland places, James, beautiful with 'green grows the rashes o',' and a little loch, clear as any well, and always, always when you lay down and drank, cool, cold, chill, and soul-restoring — now drained for the sake of marl, and forsaken by the wild swans, that used to descend from heaven in their perfect whiteness, for a moment fold up their sounding pinions, and then, hoisting their wings for sails, go veering like ships on a pleasure cruise, all up and down in every direction, obeying the air-like impulses of inward happiness, all up and down, James, such heavenly air-and-water-woven world as your own St. Mary's Loch, or Loch of the Lowes, with its old, silent, ruined chapel, and one or two shepherds' houses, as silent as the chapel, but, as you may know from the smoke, old, but not ruined, and, though silent, alive!"

Wilson frequently resorts to the dash as a mechanical contrivance for uniting the clauses of his sentences, thereby avoiding the use of conjunctions. Nevertheless, a confusion is caused by the fact that he uses these dashes both to weld together coördinate clauses, and to separate a parenthetical clause from the body of the sentence. An analysis of his long sentences usually proves them to be simple in structure; but the strain on the reader's mind is intense, and only keen sympathy with the writer's sentiments prevents them from becoming intolerably wearisome.

From excessively long sentences Wilson passes to the other extreme, and in the intoxication of some overpowering feeling, he expresses himself in short exclamations: —

"How sudden, yet how unviolent, the transitions among all our feelings! Under no other power so swift and so soft as that of Music! . . . Not a smile over all that hush. Entranced in listening, they are all still as images. A sigh — almost a sob — is heard, and there is shedding of tears." Sentences of such brevity are the outpouring of a more tumultuous and varying tempest of emotions than are the longer sentences; but they also require the strong sympathy of the reader in order to endure their abruptness. In his expository essays Wilson finds these brief ejaculations forcible in emphasizing his opinions. Scattered among more finished sentences in the essay on *Tennyson* are short sentences such as these: "Miserable indeed!" "That is drivel!"

As another sign of Wilson's attainment of clearness in his critical essays we mention the balanced and antithetical sentences. A comprehensive parallel between Burns and Johnson is embraced in a sentence four pages in length, and composed of a series of balanced statements. The following series of sentences, in addition to their balanced structure, have a repetition of the same subject at the beginning of each sentence:—

"The Young Poets, we said, all want fire. Macaulay, then, is not one of the set; for he is full of fire. The Young Poets, too, are somewhat weakly; he is strong. The Young Poets are rather ignorant; his knowledge is great. The Young Poets mumble books; he devours them. The Young Poets dally with their subject; he strikes its heart. The Young Poets twiddle on the Jew's harp; he sounds the trumpet. The Young Poets are arrayed in long singing-robes, and look like women; he chants succinct — if need be — for a charge. The Young Poets are still their own heroes; he sees but the chiefs he celebrates. The Young Poets weave dreams with shadows transitory as clouds; with substances he builds realities lasting as rocks. The Young Poets are imitators all; he is original. The Young Poets steal from all and sundry, and deny their thefts.

He robs in the face of day. Whom? Homer."

In the arbitrary selection of his sentences, his disregard of their length, and his lawless use of the dash, Wilson is not a model for any young writer. His natural genius led him usually to the most appropriate choice of sentences; his masterful feelings and his magnetic force give to them an emotional union, when, by calm analysis, there will be found no true rational unity. The great variety in the forms of his sentences are on a par with the number of his themes, the varying moods in which he composed, and the profuseness of his diction. Without these gifts his sentences would betoken lack of artistic skill; with them they betoken natural art.

PARAGRAPHS.

A more systematic disposition of paragraphs than of sentences is noticeable in Wilson's works. Again, however, we find a different degree of explicitness in his critical and rhapsodical writings. This is but natural, for, since the object of his criticisms is to throw light on various points, these elucidations group themselves into distinct paragraphs. On the other hand, his fanciful sketches, partaking of the character of monologues, are rambling and discursive, and show a less firm welding together of sentences and of paragraphs.

All the conditions necessary for a model paragraph, as enumerated by Bain, are fulfilled by Wilson in the former class of essays. (1) Very rare are the instances when each sentence does not react upon the preceding and is not acted upon by the succeeding sentence. This mutual interaction is maintained by all the legitimate modes of explicit reference;—the use of various conjunctions, pronouns, repetitions of words and inverted position of clauses. The most characteristic means of linking his sentences is through interrogatories. A series of questions is asked and followed by their answers, in order. There is likewise the same interdependence of paragraphs. The following introductory phrases and words show the diversity of his connectives. "How happened it *then*." "You will not think *these words* extravagant." "It was in *this way* that." "And *here* it is incumbent." "*However*."

(2) A striking example of parallel construction is afforded by the example of balanced clauses already cited.

(3) The opening sentence never leads one astray as to the subject of the paragraph; but rather seems to embrace the whole topic, while the sentences that follow are amplifications, reiterations or illustrations of its thought.

(4) A nicety in marking out the proper scope of each paragraph distinguishes Wilson's critical style. He rarely makes the mistake of introducing irrelevant matter, or of separating into distinct paragraphs closely related ideas. Each holds within its limits a family of ideas bound together by such close ties as not to admit of separation.

His imaginative essays, as was said before, are merely soliloquies and breezy conversations. Consequently there cannot be such unity in their paragraphs, nor such explicit connection between them. Each represents a flight of thought. The first sentence affords no clue to the purport of the paragraph; but every successive one brings with it a new surprise. We feel that the author's pen was driven along by the impetus of his emotions; he is carried away from the subject at hand by a tide of recollections suggested to him by a word; he indulges in vague and beautiful speculations; he begins with a description and ends with a long narration. All these wanderings cannot be called irrelevancies, for he seldom had in mind any definite topic. A passage on the lark in *Christopher in his Aviary* illustrates these remarks. The lark he describes calls to his mind the larks that sang in the meadows during his boyhood days. He tells us of his rambles through the "lark-loved" vales in holiday times. He thinks of one companion who was always with him. He stops to apostrophize this dear boy-friend, and to describe, with touching pathos, how he went to sea and was never heard from again. It is almost impossible to summarize such paragraphs or to point out their main trend.

FIGURES OF SPEECH.

We dignify an author with the name of poet when he addresses us in a language, not plain and direct, but beautified with figures of speech; not in the temperate words of prose, but in the tropical words of poetry. The truth must be revealed under sensuous forms. On the dividing line between prose and poetry stand many tales and essays of Wilson. They are now bright with the sparkle of his fancy, and again dark with the gloominess of his imagination. They lack but the mechanical form of poetry to transfer them to its rank.

Wilson luxuriates in that class of figures of speech which Minto designates as tropes: that is, metaphors, similes, and their closely allied figures. The most frequent of these is the personification, which likewise was most characteristic of De Quincey. He, however, employed this figure to humanize abstract ideas, while Wilson has recourse to it in humanizing objects and operations of nature. So necessary to his descriptions does this personifying element become, that when he paints a scene in ordinary descriptive language our intense interest is lost. Thence proceeds the disappointment we experience in reading the essay, *Characteristics of Highland Scenery.*

It is a favorite device of Wilson to personify the seasons of the year. His skill and originality are recognizable in these words on Spring: — "To-day, he meets you unexpectedly on the hill-side; and was there ever a face in the world so celestialised by smiles! All the features are framed of light. Gaze into his eyes, and you feel that in the untroubled lustre there is something more sublime than in the heights of the cloudless heavens, or in the depths of the waveless seas. More sublime, because essentially spiritual. There stands the young Angel, entranced in the conscious mystery of his own beautiful and blessed being; and the earth becomes all at once fit region for the sojourn of the Son of the Morning. So might some great painter image the First-born of the Year, till nations adored the picture. — To-morrow you repair, with hermit steps, to the Mount of the Vision, and, 'Fierce as ten furies, terrible as hell,' Spring clutches you by the hair with the fingers of frost; blashes a storm of sleet in your face, and finishes, perhaps, by folding you in a winding sheet of snow. . . . Hand in hand with Spring,

Sabbath descends from heaven unto earth; and are not their feet beautiful on the mountains? Small as is the voice of that tinkling bell from that humble spire, overtopped by its coeval trees, yet it is heard in the heart of infinitude. So is the bleating of these silly sheep on the braes — and so is that voice of psalms, all at once rising so spirit-like, as if the very kirk were animated, and singing a joyous song in the wilderness to the ear of the Most High."

Among his other similitudes, metaphors and similes are the most conspicuous. Occasionally he uses a metonymy with telling effect: —

"The gamester shakes his elbow, and down go the glorious oak-trees planted two hundred years ago, by some ancestor who loved the fresh smell o' the woods, — away go — if entail does no forbid — thousand o' bonny braid acres."

By elevating nature to a place in human companionship, Wilson made it a person with whom he conversed, as well as about whom he rhapsodized. Apostrophe, therefore, is almost as habitual a figure with him as personification. Its employment gave him a feeling of actual presence at the scene whereof he speaks, and afforded him a pleasant means of expressing his strong sympathies and impassioned feelings. He apostrophizes old-time friends and scenes, the great poets whom he criticizes, and all objects of external nature. Among them all shines out most brightly his passionate apostrophe to the *Evening Star:* —

"Art thou the Evening Star, sole Shiner in a sky that might have tempted out the whole starry host from the inmost heavens! Thou hast glided down, all by thyself, to take a look of this fair earth, as gradually it is growing dim in the dying day."

Closely interwoven with apostrophes are exclamations and interrogations which share in giving a natural conversational tone to his writings. What sarcasm enters into his speech is open ridicule, sharp condemnatory remarks, or, in the *Noctes*, bits of irony at the expense of himself and of the other characters in the dialogues.

He had the power to soften and embellish the form of his sarcastic remarks, while at the same time he armed them with a more biting sting. In speaking of the young poets who send their poems to *Blackwood*, he compares them to troublesome insects, and the magazine to a peerless maiden: —

"But still will they be seeking to insinuate themselves through her long deep veil, which nunlike she wears at gloaming; and can they complain of cruelty if she brush them away with her lily hand, or compress them with her snow-white fingers into unlingering death?"

Sources of Similitudes. — (1) *From Human Nature*. Wilson's live and sympathetic interest in all phases of human life afforded him a vast field from which to gather apt similitudes for his numerous descriptive sketches. He was not confined to the usual stock of comparisons between man and insensate nature, for he had met all classes of his fellow-beings; he had studied with philosophic acuteness and thoroughness their manifold emotions; he had regarded them with the prosaic eyes of an active man of the world, and with the glorified vision of the poet. The winning charm and tender human interest which similitudes of this origin impart to his essays is exemplified by his comparison between the dove and woman from *Christopher in his Aviary.*

(2) *From Feminine Beauty and Dress.* To similitudes from this source belong some of the daintiest and most novel of Wilson's figures of speech. A long line of noble similes owe their inspiration to the effect of the sensuous beauty of woman upon his artistic eye. This little one is a model of delicate coloring: —

"The same heavens! more blue than any color that tinges the flowers of the earth — like the violet veins of a virgin's bosom."

He describes Memory as one of three sisters, Memory, Imagination, and Hope: —

"Memory has deep, dark, quiet eyes, and when she closes their light, the long eyelashes lie like shadows on her pensive cheeks, that smile faintly as if the dreamer were half asleep — a visionary slumber, which sometimes the dewdrop melting on the leaf will break, sometimes not the thunder-peal with all its echoes."

He takes up some little feminine peculiarity and makes use of it in a piquant figure: —

"Never see ye her (Nature's) hair in papers, for crisp and curly, far-streamin and wide-wavin are her locks."

(3) *From Mechanical Operations.* The figures of this class are few. Their presence tends to strengthen and to condense his thought, and to hold down his too light buoyancy of imagination. As an example we quote: —

"As to Flowers, they are the prettiest periodicals ever published in folio — the leaves are *wire-wove* and *hot-pressed* by Nature's self."

(4) *From External Nature.* Wilson elevated the objects and operations of external nature by com-

parison, either formal or tacit, to human passions and works. He reverses the order and beautifies human thoughts and acts by pointing out likenesses to them in nature. His knowledge of both man and nature was wide and deep. In his heart they were closely bound together; hence the transition from one to the other was quick and easy. With poetic taste he selects birds and flowers for the majority of his similitudes. His knowledge of Natural History and his minute personal observations aided him in carrying out into detail his comparisons. He thereby invested them with a force and pertinence which they could not have in the hands of the ordinary writer. Such an author might have omitted the latter half of the following simile, which is freighted with significant meaning: —

"The dearest thocht and feelings o' auld lang syne come crowd-crowding back again into the heart whenever there's an hour o' perfect silence, just like so many swallows coming a-wing frae God knows where, when winter is ower and gane, to the self-same range o' auld clay biggins, aneath the thatch o' house, or the slate o' ha' — unforgetfu' they o' the place where they were born, and first hunted the insect-people through shadow or sunshine!"

(5) *From Objects and Conversations of Every-day Life.* Sprinkled in among his exquisitely flowery metaphors and similes is a plentiful supply of homely and most prosaically ludicrous figures: "As warm as so many pies;" "As flat as a flounder." He compares the extravagant eulogies heaped upon Tennyson to a costly gingerbread structure, frosted and covered with comfits; and again, in speaking of this same extrav-

agance of praise, he says, "none splash it on like the trowel-men who have been bedaubing Mr. Tennyson."

(6) *From Literature.* Of similitudes drawn from this source the majority are from classical authors, and the greater part of these from the *Iliad* and *Odyssey.*

Success in Fulfilling Conditions of Effective Comparison. — Figures of speech are for two purposes: (1) to afford pleasure to the reader; (2) to aid in exposition. Wilson has for his desire that which is the end of all art, to excite ennobling pleasure. In his finest similitudes he attains this object to an extraordinary degree, and in his poorest he falls far below it. The principal requisite, originality in comparison, is undeniably his possession. A vast number of his figures are children of his fertile imagination, and bear the stamp of their parentage so plainly that there can be no mistaking their birth. Others of his similitudes owe their origin to other writers. His personifications of nature show an acquaintance with Chaucer, Spenser, Milton, and Thomson. However, though these figures are not his own children, they have been adopted into the family, and not stolen. For example, in all the poets the seasons of the year are personified; but while the poets introduce them to us as mythical personages, Wilson makes of them genuine Scotch people. In other cases he follows one of these poetic figures with a homely simile which gives the whole the novel comicality characteristic of him : —

"The first September frosts chilled the rosy fingers of the Morn as she bathed them in the dews, and the air is cool as a cucumber."

Another way in which he wields an old figure with new power is shown in the following simile:—

"Man who is but grass, and like the flower of the field flourisheth and is cut down, and raked away out of the sunshine into the shadow of the grave."

By the addition of the last clause to the familiar comparison of the psalmist, he clothes it with new beauty, and brings out more forcibly the contrast between the light of life and the darkness of the grave.

Besides possessing the faculty of exhausting the points of similarity in one comparison, Wilson had also a quick facility in suggesting a variety of happy similitudes for the same object. Therefore the quality of variety in figures of speech is added to originality.

It is true that many of his figures can make no pretension to originality. But the surprise of meeting these very trite figures in a finished artistic essay is sometimes agreeable, and lends to his style a daring boldness and raciness. More often, however, the shock is a disagreeable one.

Wilson's similitudes of exposition are comparatively few. They are usually terse, simple, and clear, very seldom elaborate or startlingly novel. In all his comparisons he attained to great aptness and accuracy. When used to elevate the character of any person, they are of the most temperate and noble nature. His greatest fault lies in the coarseness of many of his similitudes employed for the purpose of ridicule.

QUALITIES OF STYLE.

SIMPLICITY.

Almost absolute simplicity is characteristic of this author's style; though not such simplicity as detracts from one's zest in perusal. He escapes abstruseness, not through a path of tame monotony, avoiding all elements constitutive of abstruseness, but by the judicious use of all artistic embellishments. His is a simplicity both of subject-matter and of mode of treatment. As a broad basis for this double simplicity we find his most deeply ingrained characteristic to be a sympathy which guided him to the choice of subjects of general human interest, and to an attractive manner of treatment. Yet his true independence of character saved him from any servility to popular opinions.

Subject-Matter. — When we consider the variety of his subjects, we are surprised that Wilson always limited their range to those which touch human thought and feeling most closely. In his tales we meet with the portrayal of such feelings as pulsate in the common tide of affairs, and with the recital of such practical details as make up this common tide. Although many of his stories have historical significance, and therefore might be more intelligible to readers of his day than to those of the present, nevertheless their political importance is but slight. We note as illustrations the tales of the Covenanters in *The Lights and Shadows of Scottish Life*. Likewise, in all essays having any reference to the political or religious affairs of his time, only such matters are treated of without explanation as are presumably within the knowledge of the most ordinary reader. The fragments of philosophic thought found in his essays and in the *Noctes* show his discrimination in detecting how far he could carry his speculations and yet be intelligible. His critical and imaginative essays deal with familiar subjects; — the lives and works of well-known poets, descriptions of ramblings and fishing excursions blended with simple stories and anecdotes.

It is much easier for the mind to grasp concrete notions than abstract. The former are prevalent in Wilson's writings. His descriptions all pertain to special persons and places. He still further particularizes by interweaving his own personal experiences with the scenes he describes. Such abstract principles as he deduces generally lapse into concrete instances.

Mode of Treatment. — Yet such simple subjects as those of Wilson's choice are capable of being shrouded in a cloak of abstruseness by their representation. We must discover in what way he still further promoted this simplicity of his style.

(1) *In Language.* It is generally conceded that words of Anglo-Saxon derivation are easier of comprehension than those of Latin origin. The greater part of Wilson's vocabulary is composed of the former and of the least pedantic of Latin derivatives. His figures of speech, as we have seen, are taken from familiar sources; therefore his frequent embellishments still preserve the simplicity of his plainer diction. The same effect is produced by his personifications of abstract ideas, through which vague notions are represented in distinct forms.

(2) The most cogent proof of Wilson's simplicity of

style is found in the fact that the perusal of his writings requires so little concentration of the mind. There is slight attempt at connection between the various rhapsodical flights, the sentence or thought immediately before one being all that calls for attention. No straining to keep in sight a distinct thread of thought is necessary, but only to experience pleasure and to derive benefit from individual pictures, stories, descriptions, and analyses.

What shall be said of his expository articles when he does call for connected thoughts? Is there any means by which he aids us in following related ideas, while our attention is not distracted from the contemplation of individual thoughts? His success is displayed in his *Essay on Burns*, where he follows out a simple and natural plan of treatment. He carries along at the same time the life, the development of character, and the writings of the poet, and thus displays their interaction; first, the events influencing his character, this in turn affecting the works of the poet, and these reacting on life and character. In this way we are easily guided through an exhaustive and critical study.

Thus his manner of treatment is suited to his subject: when the subject is simple he treats it directly; when verging on the abstruse he treats of it indirectly, disguised under simpler forms.

Defects in Simplicity. — On the other hand, there are certain attributes of Wilson's style which counteract the effect of those qualities just mentioned, and lead in the direction of abstruseness. The slang phrases and provincialisms he uses are limited in their comprehensibility to a fixed time and place. Many of them are unintelligible to readers of the present day. The Scottish element of his vocabulary is to many abstruse, but with the help of the glossary appended to most editions is easily mastered. A source of bewilderment is sometimes found in his frequent accumulations of words and clauses. His brief, concise remarks are often difficult of ready comprehension.

It often happens that the most fascinating and characteristic qualities of his style are those which cloud our vision. His eloquence and delicate fancy veil his thoughts in a mysteriousness penetrable only by another lively imagination. Such obscurities, however, are rare. Wilson deserves a high rank among simple authors, and is a model for unpretentious writers, to whom simplicity should be the paramount aim, in that he takes for his themes subjects of personal experience and current interest, and handles them with natural ease.

CLEARNESS.

Perspicuity. — Although Wilson is simple in style, he is rarely perspicuous. His lack of general clearness in the thought and outline of his essays is no defect, but only a legitimate outcome of the nature and aim of these works. Nor does the absence of perspicuity cause perplexity or confusion. It is left for the imaginative, sympathetic reader to feel rather than to perceive the connection between thoughts. Wilson indulges in an inveterate and acknowledged habit of wandering. Were there some main argument at stake, such looseness of thought would be injurious, but, as usually the avowed purpose of his essays is to amuse, they are made more novel and attractive by these digressions. A characteristic example of his deficiency in perspicuity is his paper on *Dr. Kitchiner.* In one portion he is criticising some remarks of Dr. Kitchiner on cleanliness, and after instituting a comparison between men and streams, he wanders off into a vivid little description of a stream, with apparently no bearing on the subject: —

"Some streams, just like some men, are always clean — you cannot well tell why — producible to good pic-nic society either in dry or wet weather. In dry, the pearly waters are singing among the freshened flowers — so that the trout, if he chooses, may breakfast among bees. In wet, they grow, it is true, dark and drumly — and at midnight, when heaven's candles are put out, loud and oft the angry spirit of the water shrieks. But Aurora beholds her face in the clarified pools and shallows — far and wide glittering with silver or with gold. All the banks and braes reappear green as emerald from the subsiding current — into which look with the eyes of an angler, and you behold a Fish — a twenty-pounder — steadying himself — like an uncertain shadow; and oh! for George Scougal's leister to strike him through the spine! Yes, these are the images of trees far down, as if in another world; and, whether you look up or look down, alike in all its blue, braided, and unbounded beauty, is the morning sky!"

Another tendency towards vagueness and irregularity is evinced in his long, loose sentences. That he can be perspicuous and lucid in the discussion of any vital matter he has proved in his critical essays, and in his plea for the *Education of the People.*

Minute Exactness. — We note both the presence and the absence of this element of style in Wilson's writings. He carries on a hazardous trifling with quotations from other authors, turning them so far from their original purport as to leave one in utter confusion regarding their true meaning. In his facetious play he leaves the reader to attach whatever sense he chooses to these carelessly scattered words. His humorous sketches and railing satires often contain sweeping assertions and exaggerated comparisons, which he takes no pains to corroborate: —

"Only in such prose as ours can the heart pour forth its effusions like a strong spring discharging ever so many gallons in a minute, either into pipes that conduct it through some great Metropolitan city, or into a watercourse that soon becomes a rivulet, then a stream, then a river, then a lake, and then a sea."

Or again, such a rash, unconsidered statement as the following: —

"Prose, we believe, is destined to drive what is called Poetry out of the world. . . . Milton was woefully wrong in speaking of 'prose or numerous verse.' Prose is a million times more numerous than verse."

Nevertheless, Wilson, in many cases, may compete in exactness with De Quincey himself. Our quotations of his figures of speech show that even in his lighter essays there was an inclination to carry out his comparisons to their extreme limit, and to exhaust every possible point of resemblance. His critical essays manifest the same minuteness in formal comparisons between different authors, an effort to impress us clearly with the exact points of distinction and similarity.

His treatise on *The Punishment of Death* furnishes the most remarkable example of his habit of minute exactness. It abounds in general summaries followed by all the practical details that authorize these conclusions: —

"There seem to be Three Great Causes of Inefficiency in the Laws which are framed to severity beyond the crime — their deadening the moral sense of the people — their hardening the temper of criminals — their uncertainty of execution."

After this statement he proceeds to a minute disquisition on these Three Causes. He seldom uses a comparative or superlative adjective without specifying its exact application: —

"There is one portion of our population more corrupt than the rest — which, by indigence, vice, ignorance, — abject condition of every kind, is the lowest among us."

Other examples of direct specification are numerous, such as sentences of this nature, "All these men are old in their lights."

He makes it his business many times to contradict opinions of general acceptation, and to exemplify and prove his corrections: —

"The great French Revolution, many say, made all our great English poets. It did not make Cowper, and it could not make Crabbe."

Therefore we find that we can neither designate Wilson as absolutely and preëminently clear in style, nor as ambiguous. In this respect he is changeable, and his effort to be clear is gauged by the importance of his subject. He can seldom be called truly ambiguous, on account of the native simplicity of his style.

STRENGTH.

De Quincey exalts and invigorates the mind by the elaborate and sustained dignity of his thought and speech. Wilson stimulates the brain and heart of the reader by the vigor and sparkling animation of his writings. In this he approaches nearer to Macaulay than to De Quincey, with this difference, however, between himself and Macaulay, that he possesses greater buoyancy and irregularity of style, less artificiality. In both De Quincey and Macaulay the sentiment of power awakened by their writings is partly caused by the enthusiasm we feel for their literary skill — their capability of grasping large subjects, their confident use of artistic adornments. The effect is as if we looked upon a consummate actor, in whose personality we are not so much entranced, as in what we are able to criticize and to analyze, — his artistic movements. But when reading Wilson we seem transported bodily to the scenes he describes, and the stimulus is such as would be received from actual contemplation of the objects and deeds, rather than from admiration of the author.

The animation of Wilson's style is maintained (1) by abrupt and rapid transitions of thought. Without any preparation or warning he leaps suddenly from one thought to another, from the pathetic to the humorous, from the sublime to the ludicrous. There are few long-suspended climaxes. Thus to sweep over great distances between thoughts produces in one a feeling of elation at conscious mental power, and is also creative of quick-wittedness.

(2) The vigor of Wilson's style is due to a great

extent to his choice of subjects. There is an intense animalism in all he writes. The narration of fishing and athletic sports, of Highland scenes and of conversations in convivial gatherings, brings a stimulus which can best be compared to the bracing effect of a morning walk. North is preëminent in this faculty of arousing the animal spirits, and in writings of this fervent stamp he exhibits the greatest originality of genius. The following is a typical example: —

"And oh! from the bright, balmy, blooming heather-bed, elastic in its mossy sweetness, how like a giant refreshed with mountain dew springs up the pedestrian at first touch of the morning light — from the shutting door shakes hands with the new-risen sun, nor in the bounding fever of his prime envies the rushing of the eagle's wing."

This tendency to personify, to infuse life and the highest form of life into all nature, helps to impart vigor to his style, by exciting somewhat the same active sympathy with movements of nature as with human actions. It is noticeable that there is motion in all his pictures. His descriptions of nature in repose are few, and even in them there is some covert allusion to action; such as smoke wreathing from the chimney of a cottage, which betokens life astir within.

His vividness in description constitutes another element of his strength, in that it inflames the imagination and gives it a consciousness of its power. One of his favorite and most vivid descriptions is that of a Highland thunder-storm.

We have spoken of the personifying element in his figures of speech as conducive to strength. In addition to these there are many comparisons of the forms of nature to products of human industry, which are conducive to the same result.

(3) Wilson is powerful and almost sublime in depicting horrible scenes. He often errs, however, in making his imagery so realistic that its effect is depressing rather than thrilling. Excessive vividness in such passages detracts from their strength. The shepherd's dream of a gambling hell is his happiest success in balancing the two extremes; horribly realistic imagery and vagueness in the portrayal of imaginary horrors. The following strong metaphor occurs:—

"They say that some nichts in thae Hells, when Satan and Sin sit thegither on ae chair, he wi' his arm roun' the neck o' that Destruction his daughter, a horrible temptation invades men's hearts and souls, drivin and draggin them on to the doom o' everlasting death."

(4) It is when Wilson seizes hold of real human nature, and exhibits it in its varied and interesting forms, that his style becomes most forcible and vigorous. He usually touches external nature in her brightest and most joyous moods, and seldom rises to sublimity. But he depicts human nature in its whole range of feelings, from the most passive to the most active, from the lowliest to the loftiest passions and actions.

The subjects of Wilson's critical essays are not always such authors as would inspire us with the loftiest sentiments. His criticisms of *Tennyson*, *Thomson*, *Coleridge*, and others, are stimulating only so far as they delight us by the demands upon our analytical faculties. He rises to a more exalted plane in his essays on *Burns* and *Macaulay*, and in his remarks on Dante and Petrarch in the *Loves of the Poets*, when sympathy with the author and admiration of his genius combine with our own self-conscious power of criticism.

In his bits of narration, it is true, Wilson shows a tendency to dwell on the softer and more touching feelings, — resignation, melancholy, quiet love. This is especially noticeable in the *Lights and Shadows of Scottish Life*. Yet pictures of stronger and more inspiring passions are intermingled with the others. The best known of these is probably the story of *The Eagle and Hannah Lamond's Bairn*. This narrative stands just on the border line between strength and sublimity. Its theme is sublime, — the king of birds thwarted in his cruel strength by a woman inspired with maternal love. But the sentences are too broken, and the feelings too passion-swept for true sublimity.

Wilson attains his highest degree of strength when portraying either the joyous, exulting animal spirits of youth, or some intense physical suffering. The following example displays his eloquence in the first: —

"Higher up among the rocks, and cliffs, and stones, we see a stripling, whose ambition it is to strike the sky with his forehead, and wet his hair in the misty cloud, pursuing the ptarmigan now in their variegated summer-dress, seen even among the unmelted snows."

The finest illustration of his force in describing physical suffering is the shepherd's account of his parching thirst on the desert, and his final relief.

It is seldom that Wilson can be called sublime. His facile feelings and his excited utterance forbid the exalted, sustained power necessary to uphold the sublime.

The few occasions in which he is sublime are worthy of mention. He is so when he speaks in hushed awe of the relation between God and man, and the closeness of the spiritual to the material. Also the following short passage deserves a place among his few sublime touches; it is the martyrdom of a young, fair maiden : —

"Tied to a stake on the sea-sands she stood; and first she heard, and then she saw, the white roarin o' the tide. But the smile forsook not her face; it brichtened in her een when the water reached her knee; calmer and calmer was her voice of prayer, as it beat again' her bonny breast; nae shriek when a wave closed her lips for ever; and methinks, sir — for ages on ages hae lapsed awa sin' that martyrdom, and therefore Imagination may withouten blame dally wi' grief — methinks, sir, that as her golden head disappeared, 'twas like a star sinkin in the sea."

PATHOS.

A tender and graceful style is highly characteristic of Wilson. Examples of pathos are numerous in his writings. It is his eloquent and touching pathos, as well as his rapid transitions of thought, that makes him akin to Jeremy Taylor. We have seen that Wilson was not capable of any sustained sublimity. He is capable of sustained pathos, although usually it forms but one of his many varying moods. His sparkling animal spirits either shade off into softer, calmer thoughts, or pass, by reaction, into melancholy.

The poetic qualities of his composition, his figures of speech, his musical language and alliteration are in harmony with his descriptions of the beautiful in nature, and therefore enhance their grace. Among the galaxy of these soft pictures those which gleam out with the brightest lustre are little fragments on the sky and clouds: —

"I've seen a white lace veil, sic as Queen Mary's drawn in, lyin' afloat, withouten stirrin' aboon her snawy brow, saftenin the ee-licht and its yon braided clouds, as if they had lain there all their lives."

He describes nature — the earth, the sun, and the sky — in all its most peaceful aspects. His descriptions of sunset can hardly be excelled. The following picture of dawn we select because its graceful language, delicate coloring, exquisite figures and the deep feeling of religious awe suffusing it, combine to make it one of his most characteristic sketches of the beautiful: —

"O thou first, faint, fair, finest tinge of dawning light that streaks the still-sleeping, yet just-waking face of the morn, light and no-light, a shadowy something, that as we gaze is felt to be growing into an emotion that must be either Innocence or Beauty, or both blending together into Devotion before Deity, once more duly visible in the divine coloring that forebodes another day to mortal life — before thee what holy bliss to kneel upon the greensward in some forest glade, while every leaf is a-tumble with dewdrops, and the happy little birds are beginning to twitter, yet motionless among the boughs — before Thee to kneel as at a shrine, and breathe deeper and deeper — as the lustre waxeth purer and purer, brighter and more bright, till range after range arise of crimson clouds in altitude sublime, and breast above breast expands of yellow woods softly glittering in their far-spread magnificence — then what holy bliss to breathe deeper and deeper unto Him who holds in the hollow of his hand the heavens and the earth, our high but most humble orisons! But now it is Day, and broad awake seems the whole joyful world. The clouds — lustrous no more — are all anchored on the sky, white as fleets waiting for the wind. Time is not felt — and one might dream that the Day was to endure forever. Yet the great river rolls on in the light — and why will he leave those lovely inland woods for the naked shores? Why — responds some voice — hurry we on our own lives — impetuous and passionate far more than he with all his cataracts — as if anxious to forsake the regions of the upper day for the dim place from which imagination sometimes seems to see even through the sunshine, beyond the bourne of this our unintelligible being, stretching sea-like into a still more mysterious night!"

We have said that Wilson seldom produced sustained pathos. This is true only in respect to his essays. His *Lights and Shadows of Scottish Life* is composed entirely of stories of a pathetic nature, in which youth, beauty, and innocence meet with undeserved and pitiful sorrows, or are rewarded by quiet happiness. The gentle, subdued tone of these stories, however, becomes monotonous. His pathos is more effective when it occurs in close contact with the animated, humorous, or serious.

Wilson is especially fine in his pictures of youth and old age. His character-sketches of boyhood belong to his strong passages; but in describing maidenhood he extols principally beauty and virtue. He is most attractive, however, when he slips into his soft, mellow, twilight strain, and rhapsodizes on Old Age: —

"There are lights that die not away with the dying sunbeams — there are sounds that cease not when the singing of birds is silent — there are motions that still stir the soul . . , and therefore how calm, how happy, how reverend, beneath unoffended Heaven, is the head of Old Age."

In Scotch pathos Wilson surpasses all essayists, and is only equalled by the poet Burns. Scottish words from their association and musical ring are peculiarly fitted for pathos; as, "wee bit bairnie," "sae lang sin syne," "a bit white breaking wave" or "silly sea-bird." His descriptions of the Saturday Eve and Sunday of the Cotter are only comparable in quaint simplicity to Burns's "Cotter's Saturday Night." He also resembles that poet in his tender love romances and in his sympathetic descriptions of dumb animals. .

His reminiscences of old friends are always tender, and his fragments on filial affection and religious sentiment are exquisitely delicate. The following passage is a poetical exposition of true friendship: —

"In utter prostration, and sacred privacy of soul, I almost think now, and have often felt heretofore, man may make a confessional of the breast of his brother man. . . . One such friend alone can ever, from the very nature of things, belong to any one human being, however endowed by nature and beloved of Heaven. He is felt to stand between us and our upbraiding conscience. In his life lies the strength — the power — the virtue of ours, — in his death the better half of our whole being seems to expire. Such communion of spirit, perhaps, can only be in existences rising towards their meridian; as the hills of life cast longer shadows in the westering hours, we grow — I should not say more suspicious, for that may be too strong a word — but more silent, more self-wrapt, more circumspect — less sympathetic even with kindred and congenial natures, who will sometimes, in our almost sullen moods or theirs, seem as if they were kindred and congenial no more — less devoted to Spirituals, that is, to Ideas, so tender, true, beautiful, and sublime, that they seem to be inhabitants of heaven though born of earth, and to float between the two regions angelical and divine — yet felt to be mortal, human still — the Ideas of passions and desires, and affections, and 'impulses that come to us in solitude,' to whom we breathe out our souls in silence or in almost silent speech, in utterly mute adoration, or in broken hymns of feeling, believing that the holy enthusiasm will go with us through life to the grave, or rather knowing not, or feeling not, that the grave is anything more than a mere word with a somewhat mournful sound, and that life is changeless, cloudless, unfading as the heaven of heavens, that lies to the uplifted fancy in blue immortal calm, round the throne of the eternal Jehovah!"

Although Wilson shows so much of the "Celtic Magic" in his natural descriptions, that is, the power to make Nature appear in a mystic, weird light, his sad pathos has none of the melancholy, despairing "Celtic Grief," that comes without any cause. He is not morose, but only breaks out into words of sorrow at the thought of some human grief. In the tearfully pathetic he is most happy when he describes or narrates the sorrows that come upon youth and innocence. Death is so beautified by his delicacy of language, and his avoidance of all that is repulsive, as to form the pleasing theme of many artistic sketches. The following quotation will afford one a just estimate of his skill in this particular: —

"In the silence, sobs and sighs, and one or two long, deep groans! Then in another moment, he saw, through the open door of the room where Lucy used to sleep, several figures moving to and fro in the light, and one figure upon its knees — who else could it be but her father! Unnoticed he became one of the pale-faced company — and there he beheld her on her bed, mute and motionless, her face covered with a deplorable beauty — eyes closed, and her hands clasped upon her breast! 'Dead, dead, dead,' muttered in his ringing ears a voice from the tombs, and he fell down in the midst of them with great violence upon the floor."

THE LUDICROUS.

Humor. — Whether Wilson excels in pathos or in humor has often formed a subject of dispute. So rare is his skill in both that those natures most susceptible to the tender and sad laud him as their master of pathos; while those, on the other hand, who are keenly sensitive to the ludicrous, are as strong in their praises of his unique humor. He said it was his delight to brood over both the pathetic and ludicrous, and to pass from the one to the other at will. The wonderful power of the pathos in his writings gives us good reason to expect an equally delicate and forcible humor; for the true, warm sympathies that produced the one, would, by their nature, beget the second. As Carlyle says, "The essence of humor is sensibility; warm, tender fellow-feeling for all forms of existence."

The close relation between his pathos and humor is shown by the many instances in which the pathetic glistens out suddenly into the ludicrous, and the humorous melts away into the pathetic. Convincing examples are found in *Christmas Dreams* and in his *Rhapsodies on the Seasons*. This perpetual interchange of pathos and humor has a twofold beneficial nature: (1) it prevents him from indulging in maudlin sentiment; (2) it restrains him from a tendency towards coarseness and buffoonery in his witty sallies.

Wilson's humor is often of a homely nature, and enjoyable because of its homeliness. He possesses the peculiar gift of caricaturing common, every-day events, ludicrous and embarrassing situations, duties and discomforts that can be made irksome or laughable, as one chooses. He is ridiculing the exaggerated way in which people talk of the pleasure of living at home, and says: —

"People seldom live very well at home. There is always something requiring to be eaten up, that it may not be lost, which destroys the soothing and satisfactory symmetry of an unexceptionable dinner."

The same laughable, good-natured ridicule is used in *Cottages*, and also in the *Essay on Early Rising*, which is perhaps one of the most truly ludicrous of his essays.

There is a freshness and joyousness about Wilson's humor, and a pleasant assumption of sharing in the human frailties he ridicules, which relieves him of all unpleasantness. One of his most charming bits of pleasantry is the following quotation: —

"Gallantry forbids, but Truth demands to say, that young ladies are but indifferent sketchers. The dear creatures have no notion of perspective. At flower-painting and embroidery, they are pretty fair hands, but they make sad work among waterfalls and ruins. Notwithstanding, it is pleasant to hang over them, seated on stone or stool, drawing from nature; and now and then to help them in with a horse or a hermit. It is a difficult, almost an impossible thing — that foreshortening. The most speculative genius is often at a loss to conjecture the species of a human being foreshortened by a young lady. The hanging Tower of Pisa is, we believe, some thirty feet or so off the perpendicular, and there is one at Caerphilly about seventeen; but these are nothing to the castles in the air we have seen built by the touch of a female magician; nor is it an unusual thing with artists of the fair sex to order their plumed chivalry to gallop down precipices considerably steeper than a house, on animals apparently produced between the tiger and the bonassus.... Nevertheless, we repeat, that it is delightful to hang over one of the dear creatures, seated on stone or stool, drawing from nature; for whatever may be the pencil's skill, the eye may behold the glimpse of a vision whose beauty shall be remembered when even Windermere himself has for a while faded into oblivion."

The vein of humor running through the *Noctes* comes out plainly in his imitation of De Quincey's pedantic style of conversation.

Wit.— During those years of hot political strife in England and in Scotland, many biting satires came from Wilson's pen. In his witty sallies and railleries he impaled his victims with merciless cruelty. He ridiculed and degraded them by exaggerating their defects, by causing them to play ludicrous parts in his allegories, by using slang phrases. A favorite and peculiar method of his was to assume an air of lofty superiority, and to treat his antagonists as mere pigmies, with whom he played in a leonine fashion. The bitterness of his wit has been tempered to us by the intervening lapse of time. The impression it makes is one of mingled pleasure and indignation; the latter at seeing the strong in the act of crushing the weak.

Wilson is too open in his ridicule ever to be malignant. Although his wit is generally delicate and fanciful, it sometimes verges on coarseness and contumely. This is especially the case when he was provoked by what seemed to him a sham poet or artist. At such times he became flippant and impertinent. Many examples can be found in his essays on *Homer and his Translators* and on *Tennyson*. In criticising the *Lotus Eaters* he says:—

"The vessel in which the land-lubbers were drifting when the Sea-Fairies salute them with a song, must have been an old tub of a thing, unfit even for a transport."

Wilson's humorous writings are crowded with witticisms of a trifling nature, such as the clever turning of quotations from their original meaning, puns, and epigrams.

Melody and Harmony.—The music in Wilson's prose is so clear and distinct that the most uncultivated ear can detect it; and it has procured for him a distinguished place among melodious and artistic writers. There seems to be no technical term by which to designate his melody. It has no alliance whatever with the stately march either of De Quincey or of Macaulay. As Minto compared the music of De Quincey's prose to the "swell and crash of an organ," so we might liken Wilson's to a Scotch ballad sung by a human voice or by a violin. The oft-recurring strain is simple, touching, and sweet. The effect is heightened by the alliteration of pleasant consonant sounds, by the repetition of vowel sounds, and by his choice of musical English and Scotch words.

In his most deeply impassioned moods the musical ring and rhythm of his utterances is most distinct. Consequently we should look among his descriptions and reminiscences of Scottish life for a typical example of melody. It is also there that we find the most sympathetic and delicate harmony between the words and the subject-matter. His poetic temperament and natural love of music insured for him a musical flow in the sincere and natural expression of his feelings. The following extract is from *Christopher in his Sporting Jacket:* —

"But oh! that Craig-Hall hawthorn! and oh! that Craig-Hall broom! They send their sweet rich scent so far into the hushed air of memory, that all the weary worn-out weaknesses of age drop from us like a garment, and even now the flight of that swallow seems more aërial — more alive with bliss his clay-built nest — the ancient long-ago blue of the sky returns to heaven — not for many a long year have we seen so fair — so frail — so transparent and angel-mantle-looking a cloud!"

Taste. — Many of the quotations already cited are sufficient to prove that Wilson possessed an innate sense of the beautiful, and a delicate artistic judgment. However, his writings have too much the character of spoken thought not to have lead him into transgressions of the artistic rules of composition. Defects of this kind are all owing to his impetuous, passionate nature, and to his hurried, careless manner of writing. We have already mentioned the most important of these violations of art principles. To summarize, they are slang words and phrases, unwieldy sentences, coarse figures of speech, scathing invectives, and boisterous humor. These faults taint but certain portions of his work; therefore those portions alone are to be condemned, and to be denied a name among works of standard literature. The main body of his works is pure in sentiment and artistic in form.

KINDS OF COMPOSITION.

DESCRIPTION.

External Nature. — With the name of Wilson is indissolubly associated the beauty and charm of Scottish Highland scenery. Not until William Black do we find any one who approaches him in picturing that country, and their manner of description is entirely unlike. How is it that Wilson has gained such fame as a descriptive writer? It is not that he has any clear and concise method of description; for, by an analysis of those works where it were natural to look for some such plan or ground-work of description, we find an entirely arbitrary mode of procedure. The delight created in us by his pictures must be accounted for otherwise than by system and order. The source of his winsomeness is found in the intense feeling breathed into and through his sketches of nature, and in the felicities of his speech.

His descriptions of external nature are usually connected with some sentiment or thought. He loves the beautiful places of this earth because they are the scene of human joys and sorrows, and because they are suggestive in their varied aspects of the different phases of human nature. His frequent personifications speak this feeling of a bond of sympathy between man and nature. His descriptions are limited to such portions of Scotland as he had visited many times and had grown intimately acquainted with. On account of this limitation, the spirit in which he writes is more enthusiastic. He is rich in the store of personal memories clustered around the scenes he describes: —

"Ye fields, that long ago we so often trode together, with the wind-swept shadows hovering about our path — Ye streams, whose murmur awoke our imaginations, as we lay reading, or musing together in day-dreams, among the broomy braes — Ye woods, where we started at the startled cushat, or paused, without a word, to hear the creature's solitary moans and murmurs deepening the far-off hush, already so profound — Ye moors and mosses, black yet beautiful, with your peat-trenches over-shadowed by the heather-blossoms that scented the wilderness afar — where the little maiden, sent from the shieling on errands to town or village in the country below, seemed, as we met her in the sunshine, to rise up before us for our delight, like a fairy from the desert bloom — Thou loch, remote in thy treeless solitude, and with nought reflected in thy many-springed waters but those low pastoral hills of excessive green, and the white-barred blue of heaven — no creature on its shores but our own selves, keenly angling in the breezes, or lying in the shaded sunshine, with some book of old ballads, or strain of some Immortal yet alive on earth — one and all bear witness to our undying affection, that silently now feeds on grief!"

The blending of these recollections with scenes of nature is not conducive to clearness or vividness; but it does increase one's interest, and thereby spur on the imagination to picture the scene for itself.

He seldom describes any place or object without mentioning the associated feelings; that is, he is seldom what is called purely descriptive: — "A pensive shade has fallen across May-day." "A Sabbath stillness is in the air." "On such days suicides rush to judgment." "It is a cloudy but not a stormy day."

(1) These associated feelings and circumstances add to the charm, but not to the vividness of his descriptions. His success in pictorial art is dependent upon other characteristics. In analyzing his descriptions to discover these characteristics we are obliged to confront the fact that he violates the chief rule; — to include with the enumeration of the parts a comprehensive statement, or general plan of the whole. He makes up for this lack of an introductory, comprehensive statement, by the suggestiveness of his pictures. He dashes on bright bits of color, and makes minor trifles conspicuous: "the blue eye of a violet looking up from the ground," "the sheep-nibbled grass, smooth as silk," "the far-off song of the cushat," or "a child shaking his sunny curls in

glee." In a few expressive words such details are mentioned; and from these the reader imagines the scene for himself. Therefore picturesqueness is the first element of his pictorial success.

(2) The second element is "Celtic Magic," as described by Matthew Arnold. It is the power to infuse into nature a life, mystic and supernatural. Wilson produces this effect when he speaks of a "knoll, whispering and quivering through the twilight with a few birches whose stems glitter like silver pillars in the shade."

(3) Wilson understands the art of individualizing his descriptions. He is careful to designate the season of the year, and often the time of day, when any particular scene was witnessed. A fine example of his power in individualizing pictures is the Shepherd's description of Noon Hour, in the valleys of Scotland.

(4) The peculiarly delicate words he uses in description we have already noted in speaking of his Vocabulary. His exquisite exactness in the adaptation of words to objects atones for all irregularity and carelessness in his mode of procedure.

(5) We have said that Wilson possesses no plan of description. He sometimes makes an exception by proceeding, for a short period, according to the Traveller's point of view. We find several examples in his Remarks on the Scenery of the Highlands, where he approaches the nearest to pure description. We quote one passage: —

"The moor is crossed, and you prepare to scale the mountain in front, for you imagine the torrent by your side flows from a tarn in yonder cove, and forms that series of waterfalls. You have been all along well pleased with the glen, and here at the head, though there is a want of cliffs of the highest class, you feel nevertheless that it has a character of grandeur. Looking westward, you are astounded to see them ranging away on either side of another reach of the glen, terrific in their height, but in their formation beautiful, for like the walls of some vast temple they stand, roofed with sky. Yet they are but as a portal or gateway of the glen. For entering in with awe, that deepens, as you advance, almost into dread, you behold, beyond, mountains that carry their cliffs up into the clouds, seamed with chasms, and hollowed out into coves, where night dwells visibly by the side of day; and still the glen seems winding on beneath a purple light, that almost looks like gloom."

Human Nature. — On account of Wilson's warm human sympathies, we expect to find in his writings many descriptions of human feelings. Such there are, and we notice in them this characteristic. He deals with external appearances and visible results of certain feelings. Like De Quincey, he arrives at motives by close inspection of every expression of the face and every action. He thus depicts the resigned grief of a mourning family: —

"Another hour of trial passed, and the child was still swimming for its life. The very dogs knew there was grief in the house, and lay without stirring, as if hiding themselves, below the long table at the window. One sister sat with an unfinished gown on her knees, that she had been sewing for the dear child, and still continued at the hopeless work, she scarcely knew why: and often,

often, putting up her hand to wipe away a tear. 'What is that?' said the old man to his eldest daughter: 'What is that you are laying on the shelf?' She could scarcely reply that it was a ribbon and an ivory comb that she had brought for little Margaret, against the night of the dancing-school ball. And at these words the father could not restrain a long, deep, and bitter groan; at which the boy, nearest in age to his dying sister, looked up weeping in his face; and, letting the tattered book of old ballads, which he had been poring on, fall out of his hands, he rose from his seat, and, going into his father's bosom, kissed him, and asked God to bless him; for the holy heart of the boy was moved within him; and the old man, as he embraced him, felt that, in his innocence and simplicity, he was indeed a comforter." This is a typical example of the great stress Wilson placed upon actions as expressive and indicative of the feelings.

Although Wilson was a philosopher, there is very little of metaphysical analysis in his descriptions of human feelings. Neither does he trace the gradual development of traits of character. He can give a wonderfully true and vivid account of some manifestation of anger or of jealousy; but he never attempts to trace the birth of these passions in others of less ugliness, and their gradual development into worse passions. His power lies in the individualization of his descriptions, in his vivid pictures of certain feelings in play rather than in an abstract treatment of these. He greatly adds to the force of his descriptions by his original and striking figures of speech.

In the delineation of character he describes by means of outward signs:—"You see at once that the man who lives here, instead of being sick of the world, is attached to all elegant socialities and amities; that he uses silver cups instead of maple bowls, shows his scallop-shell among other curiosities in his cabinet, and will treat the passing pilgrim with pure water from the spring, if he insists upon that beverage, but will first offer him a glass of the yellow cowslip-wine, the cooling claret, or the sparkling champagne."

He seldom gives any comprehensive statement of the character of his heroes, but leaves the reader to build it up for himself out of the narration of his actions. He seldom indulges in speculation or minute analysis when setting before us the characters of celebrated men. He dwells on their most familiar characteristics, and to bring these out forcibly uses all his literary skill in telling figures of speech, and in daring hyperbole.

NARRATIVE.

Wilson wrote no sustained historical work. The nearest approach to true narrative, that is, to a systematic account of events, is the biographical portion of his essay on Burns. After extricating this from the critical analysis, we find even then no remarkable display of methodical skill in narration. He obeys the first principle of narration by following the order of events from the childhood of Burns to his death. At the same time he is wise in his selection of the most important and significant of these events, and clear and penetrating in his philosophical explanations of their relations to Burns' character and genius. Another notable characteristic is his frequent interspersion of concise summaries. In his recital he stops for a moment, and to make sure that the reader is ready to continue with him, he condenses into a few words all the preceding details, then makes a fresh beginning. He thus summarizes Burns' childhood: — "His childhood, then, was a happy one, secured from all evil influences and open to all good, in the guardianship of religious parental love." His return to Mossgiel is introduced with these words: — "Burns has now got liberated, for ever, from stately 'Edinburgh throned on crags,' the favoured abode of philosophy and fashion, law and literature, reason and refinement, and has returned again into his own natural condition, neither essentially the better nor the worse of his city life; the same man he was when 'the poetic genius of his country found him at the plough and threw her inspiring mantle over him.'"

His references to past events are frequent when endeavoring to bring out forcibly some particular point: —

"And here we ask you who may be reading these pages to pause for a little, and consider with yourselves, what up to this time Burns had done to justify the condemnatory judgments that have been passed on his character as a man by so many admirers of his genius as a poet?"

These are the only laws of narrative obeyed in this biography. Its end of instruction and interest is attained otherwise, through picturesque effects, touching scenes, and philosophical comments. We have no means by which to discover whether Wilson was capable of writing a scientific history; for in a biography the writer does not meet with the same necessity of systematizing. There are not so many contemporaneous events to relate, nor such complexity in any particular subject.

Wilson's narration of simple tales possesses a peculiar charm due to its easy and graceful style. His essays are composed mainly of descriptions and narrations, and he has written a whole volume of Scotch stories. These imaginative tales do not make instructive studies in the science of narrative excepting as models of delicate beauty and simplicity. There is no intricacy of plot requiring skilful manipulation of many different incidents. There is but one simple theme in each story; one absorbing event, sometimes intensely thrilling and again pathetic or humorous. The only concurring streams of events that he has to follow are the operations of nature and the actions of human beings, and, although the due subordination of the one to the other would seem extremely simple, Wilson often goes astray by giving too great prominence to the one or the other in the inappropriate place. The characters of his stories are few, and therefore only such as play important parts. The emotions that direct their actions are natural and familiar. Since interest in Wilson's narratives is not sustained by a systematic ordering of important events, or by a skilful dramatic plotting, we are convinced that he owes his power as a narrator to his felicities of style. These are eloquence, wit, pathos, conversational ease, metaphorical and musical language.

EXPOSITION.

Wilson could scarcely be called a successful expositor. We should not consult him for information on any particular subject, unless it were to find a clear criticism of some author. The graces of his style, which we have already studied, are such as to lead him away from exposition into other fields. His glittering brilliancy of language and of thought, together with his imaginative speculations, detract from the solid worth of all his philosophical papers.

By exposition we mean a systematic treatment of a certain subject with the primary aim of instructing. Of this we find but few examples in Wilson, although we do meet with wise and beautiful thoughts and opinions strewn through his essays, and presented in fascinating forms. He gives us instruction in Natural History in *Christopher in his Aviary*. His expository essays are confined entirely to critical analyses of authors. Not all of his critical essays would come under this head, for some are merely rambling dissertations. In others, however, his diction is plain, and his mode of treatment direct and simple.

His essay on *Burns* is his best example of exposition. In it he seems not to appreciate the benefit of frequent iteration in making a subject clear. The only way in which he repeats is by summaries. In general he passes from one statement to another, trusting to the simplicity and clearness of each statement without repetition. In this particular he resembles De Quincey.

' In like manner he seldom resorts to the statement of the counter-proposition for the sake of emphasis. His nearest approach to this is shown in the following sentence:—

"*So far from detracting from the originality of his lyrics*, this impulse to composition greatly increased it, while it gave to them a more touching character than perhaps ever could have belonged to them, had they not breathed at all of antiquity."

In comparison with his usual flowery language there seems a poverty of figures of speech in these expository essays. But a close examination proves that they are frequent, but more modest than his customary figures, and in this respect appropriate to serious subjects. They are apt, concise, and elucidatory.

The new charm which he can impart to an old subject is made evident in the *Noctes*. These dialogues, however, cannot be called works of exposition, because they touch upon so many unallied themes at random, and treat none exhaustively. Whatever instruction the reader gains clings to him, without any effort of his own, by reason of its novelty, its graceful beauty or sympathetic association. It is in this pleasant way that Wilson best performs his part of expounding and teaching.

PERSUASION.

Wilson displays his oratorical powers in numerous passages. Indeed, all his essays are persuasive in that they fill us imperceptibly, by their own beauty and sincerity, with love and reverence for the beautiful and good. Instead of a disquisition on obedience to conscience and its good results, we find a passage conveying this sentiment: —

"But a still, small voice is heard within my heart — the voice of conscience — and its whispers shall be heard when all the waters of the earth are frozen into nothing, and earth itself shrivelled up like a scroll."

In the two essays *On the Punishment of Death* and *The Education of the People* he seeks to persuade by logical reasoning. He moves the understanding by a clear statement of facts and by a reasonable deduction of results from known causes. There are no highly colored pictures nor exaggerated speech such as are usually characteristic of Wilson.

His art of persuasion, however, is most irresistible in its power when addressed to the feelings. The causes of his success are:—

(1) *Intense Absorption in the Subject.* Enthusiasm calls forth enthusiasm. He seeks to persuade only in matters that come near to his heart; as in the *Lights and Shadows of Scottish Life* and in many essays where he preaches loyalty to the Scottish Highlanders.

(2) *Intense Sympathy.* This lies at the foundation of all his literary success.

(3) *Felicities of Style.* The most effective in persuasion are copiousness and vividness of illustration.

(4) *Indirect Methods of Persuasion.* He never exhibits his intention to persuade, but wins us over to his opinions through some charming narrative or choice description.

As a political leader his influence was transient. The reasons for this are the one-sided and prejudiced nature of his arguments and his free use of sarcasm and invective.

www.ingramcontent.com/pod-product-compliance
Lightning Source LLC
Chambersburg PA
CBHW020325090426
42735CB00009B/1404